T0197371

A Slice of
Grimsthorpe
Heaven

PART ONE

Candy Adderley-Dawe

AuthorHouse™ UK
1663 Liberty Drive
Bloomington, IN 47403 USA
www.authorhouse.co.uk
UK TFN: 0800 0148641 (Toll Free inside the UK)
UK Local: 02036 956322 (+44 20 3695 6322 from outside the UK)

Because of the dynamic nature of the Internet, any web addresses or links contained in this book may have changed
since publication and may no longer be valid. The views expressed in this work are solely those of the author and do not
necessarily reflect the views of the publisher, and the publisher hereby disclaims any responsibility for them.

Any people depicted in stock imagery provided by Getty Images are models,
and such images are being used for illustrative purposes only.
Certain stock imagery © Getty Images.

This book is printed on acid-free paper.

ISBN: 978-1-7283-7404-8(sc)
ISBN: 978-1-7283-7403-1 (e)

Print information available on the last page.

Published by AuthorHouse 07/07/2022

authorHOUSE®

For B Bubbles

I am so happy you exist.

To everyone else may your faith in the universe
make your dreams come through too.

Other Books By Author

Not by Bread Alone

The Good Neighbor

If She Had Only Said Sorry

So You Want To Return To Nursing

The Lost Remnants

I wrote all of the following poems summer of 2021, when I felt alone but yet so strongly attached to God and in lined with my destiny and all that creation stood for. The poems and tears poured out of me like water so did my past failings and history of short comings as I wandered like a lost yet found child around Grimsthorpe Castle, Lincolnshire. Beauty so poignant, memories so magical, words so alluring and staff so friendly couldn't help but to bring me back to my epicenter again. For every walk around the lake and grounds and hedge I sat up against to have cake I say thank you. A hundred million times, thank you.

This book is for you too trying to find your back to your epicenter.
God bless you.

Freckled Apple

Imperfections doesn't begin or
End in spots.
I think not.
I think when God made the
World
He left imperfections on
Purpose.
Marks in a perfect fruit
To show that imperfection
Merely ends and begins with God.
Freckled apple
I take the view
That it is in the crisp shot of
Over ripeness of the skin
That true beauty begins.
And that far from taking fright
The imperfection of beauty
Beckons a welcoming
Bite.

I take the view that paradise
Can be akin to bliss.
I take the view that something
Marvelous can always
Come through
When sun tickle toes.
I don't suppose it gets any
Better by
Exclamation of a wetter water
Foundation just because
The heat has been notched
Up a degree or two.
Warmly kissed toes,
God bless you 😉

I like to lean up against a
Hedge or two.
I've got no mind to alter
My position or change my
Stance,
Or even throw a glance
At the passerby who
Comes chattering through.
I like to be taken aback
Slightly slack
As my head hits the leaves
And I admire its sheaves
As I would a pillow or
Beanbag.
I do not shirk away from its
Gaze or hazy days
Spent doing nothing else
But resting up against its
Comfortable arms
And heavenly charms.
I do like a hedge or two – when
One's left with nothing
To do but nap.

(this was the last poppy of the season just as
you leave the walled kitchen garden
And enter the orchard…poppy behind barbed wire to your right)

O wrinkled poppy dear,
You wear your petals
Like a flamenco queen
Or better yet a ballroom dancer!
Shades of hazel red
So fiery – you should
Be nestled next to a weeping
Willow or a
Begrudging foxglove.

(the rock trough surrounded by lavender as you enter the orchard
From the walled kitchen garden unlatched)

I still like you, craggy
Crest and all and
In the fall when your beauty
Fade and the frost and
View suffers a little bit
Of a spade, I shall adore
You even better still.
Then cut in stems for a
Bespoken window sill.
I shall love you still.

If they mean to rip my
Heart from my chest
They are wrong.
I ripped it from my own
Chest
Awhile back
To give to another.
And he hasn't given
It back
Yet either
Though he had no use
For it.
If they mean to make me cry,
They can't
He's already drained all
Of my tear ducts too.
Whatever this is that
Remains

Is held together by duct
Tape and the word
Of God.
So let's try this again
In the beginning
It was a sin to give
One's heart to anyone
But God.
So yes I go rip
It from him:
And give it back to God
So there you see
Finally
It has a resting home – my heart
And sweet justice is done.
Broken it is not
And shall never be
Again!

24/08/2021

Frustration
Aggravation
You keep that
It's not my pathway to peace.
Gloom. Doom.
That wants to enter my home,
You keep that too.
It looks no way like nirvana
The swirling and twirling
And emotions
Swarming within
This may seems like a bargain
And the off load of my sins
But could you please have
Those too?
I'm trying to find the pathway to
Peace
The good life
Land without strife and pain
Is there such a gain or was it
My lack of reality
That led to my acute
Psychotic breakdown?
I find myself now.

Please enter the peace
the madness and sadness
Please enter the joy
And increase my gladness,
So that my heart can feel
Whole again.
It currently feels as if the
Soul
Is being ripped out.
Please enter the peace
Into my silence and gloom
Please increase the joy
In my heart and in
My home.
So I can find a sense of
Security and belonging
Again.
Please say it was not a sin
For allowing such
Things to have such
Prevalence in my heart in
The first place.

(For Grimsthorpe)

Loving you comes easy to
Me.
It's in the softness
of your branches
and the shadow of your leaves.
It's in the way the light
Plays across the dark
On a sunny summer's afternoon
On the grass.
It's in the way the water
Fountain sings
When no ones watching
It's in all these little things
about you.
That makes loving you
So very easy to me.

The body hath but two
Eyes
And the soul one
Mines ends with your
Beginning
And restarts with the sun.
Mines in the golden sunset
That shimmers across
Your lake.
Mines is just yours for yours
Alone
And keeping for keeping sake.
Mines is the million handshakes
And strokes along
Each rose.
The endless cup of teas and
Cake
That sweetens love's nature
Pose.
The body hath but one soul
I am but done
One look at you, you stole
My breath
And that was half the fun.

I like to walk with you
In you
And around you.
I like to admire your leafy
Bosoms and
Upstretched arms.
I like to see what I see every time
I see you
I like the in and out of you.
I like the alignment of
Your swan's neck
And beady necklaces on
Glistening water.
I like calves coming
up close.
And sunshine heralding
My view.
I like what you're coming
To
Or about
Every time I walk with you.

To Grimsthorpe

I can't bear it when we're
Apart
When you do your thing
And I must do mines.
Alone.
Separately – Torn apart
I like doing this and that
With you
Together.
Pulled close
Sucked in
Like the very air you breathe.
Or the sunlight poking
Through your leafy
Trees.
I like everything about you.
Notwithstanding the
View
Of being absent from you.
Or you being absent from
Me either
It pains me.
The very separation of you.

My dear Grimsthorpe
Every time I think of
You
I see poetry.
Line upon line
Stencil upon stencil
The magic of you.
Calming beauty
Stillness upon water
You can feel it in the
Air
And the atmosphere too.
There's just no stopping
You
Or withholding all your
Due.
You're awe and
Splendor
Past history and
The present
Shining through
You gave me goosebumps,
When you gave me
You.

I'm sorry if this
Relationship is
A little bit one sided.
I'm sorry if I pair more
Than my fair share
On you
Of my ravings and cravings
And groaning and moaning
To restore all that's
Right back into my world
Again.
More than you have need to
Hear or can even
Spare.
But what is sharing
Amongst trees
When the word whispers
Through the leaves and
Tell me everything
Will be okay.
And even if it's not
You're still hot
Baby. Thank you.

26/8/2021

Still mining for gold I see.
The little bits of heart
That still can and
Do respond to pain.
I see I am a blot
that even time
Hasn't forget
And the present and future will
Remember again
and again.
I see you're out after
The biggest artery and the
Juiciest vein.
How many more ores will you try?
How many capillaries?
Till tis enough.
You're satisfied. They're satisfied.
Until it's done.
But I see you're still having
Fun, and I must
Recede further into my primary core
Until your oreing is done.

27/08/2021

Joy settles on me slowly
Like peace.
On all my parched places.
Like a luxurious drink of
Water
One small sip at a
Time but quenches
My thirst
I regardless.
Joy settles on me
Peacefully
Slowly, thankfully
I welcome it in.

I like your back ways (Grimsthorpe Castle)
And alleyways
And driving to you
The expense of the
Road.
Anticipation of the view.
You cure my sadness
And mend my broken heart
Too.
You're like a balm in Gideon
When nothing else
Will do.
You've got a presence about
You
That lets the light through
And let the soul expand,
You're the width and depth
And beauty of man.
You're pure oxytocin
You carve out moments
Where
One can simply be one with nature.
And pretend that all is fair
(in love and war).

Love is where love
Should be
Love is how love should
Be.
Burning rubber and tires
For each other.
Eating up the miles
Just to be near each other.
Love is when love should
Be.
Love is where love should
Be.
Where she said she'll
Always be
If I turned up too late
Or early in excitement
Love is exactly how love
Should be
Triumphantly
Reigning for
Each other.
And thank God for that too.

What can you do with me
Dear Lord?
What can you rustle
Up with my left overs?
You told your disciples
To pick up everything
So that there was nothing
Wasted.
What will you do with my leftovers?
What flavor
My 'stone soup'?
What can you make, design
What masterpiece
Out of my broken dreams and
Life?
Out of my love lost and
Misdirection and all
My hoping and yearning too?
Can you still make 'stone soup' ?
What of my left overs Lord?
It is you, dear Lord

It is you.
And I can already feel
My new heart, hope
And spirit
Shining through
All ready and willing
To love, worship
And serve you.
So what of my leftovers
Lord,
What can you do?
What can you see through
All this mess
And I confess
I won't know what to
Do with it either.

Time to move on.
Time to slowly go
To new horizons and
Where the trees
Beckon and why.
Time for new enclosed
Spaces
And no guesses as to who
Left the glasses on the
Window sill this time
(only me or my kids)
Time to begin life anew
A fresh start.
An uprooting
Then a dawn setting
Time for a fresh view
At an old concept
Moving
To greater glory, inner
Peace
Belonging, settling
Time to move on within and
Around me.
Welcome slowly emerging you.

There's always joy in a good
Book if you
Care to look or read
Long enough.
There's always joy in a
Good read
If you succeed in
Getting from beginning
To end.
Chapter to chapter.
Cover to cover
Only to discover
You'll love to read
It again.

29/08/21

I have to find joy in the little
Things now.
Something you must
Have said
Or done
While trying to thread out the
Sadness and
Moments of regret
Made me fret.
I must find joy in the small
Things now
For the big ones are few
And far between
But more sustainable in
The longer run
To get me over the bumpy patch
The rustle of a newspaper
The joy of a good book
Shimmer of gold on a lake
And the way nature looks
Every time

I take a walk
Outside.
I take comfort in
Trees and
Uncurling of young leaves
In the spring
I take joy in everything
From a rice grain
To the flicker of pain that
Sometimes cut
Across my train of thought.
I take joy in being here
And now
And anyhow if it
Doesn't work out
Can't we start all over
Again?
Somewhere else
Like the nomads do.
Is there simply no getting
Over you?
Yes there is in life.
And that's why to lessen
The pain with the passage
Of time
I take joy as a new toy
In little things.

I watch you my son
Growing up
Your cup filled up as it
Should be
Of life and joy and
Adventures all spread
Out like a boy
Entering the world
Youth on its heel.
No-one to reveal the
Dangers lurking
Behind a corner
Except God who's already
Gone ahead to
Prepare the way for you.
I see you my son.
And you make me
Happy too.
Joy in creation and
The pride to keep going
Through again and again
The beauty and triumphs
Of life.
Happy birthday to you.
My son.

Your rays hits my toes
And I know the way
Happiness goes
Straight back home to
You.
It's true.
And you know it too.
Happiness comes back to
You.
Colour me grey away
Happiness comes back
To you.
Everything I say, I say
It with truth
Happiness comes back home
To you.
O sunny day, what
Makes me behave
This way
Happiness hits my toes and
Sunshine and golden sun knows
Yes you know it goes
Yes happiness comes back
Home to you.

To a Sunny Day
07/09/21

I love you
Already
But you know that.
You know I find your blue skies
Irresistible and
Your white clouds even
More so.
I don't know where I'll go
Without you.
You're pure sunshine
Through and through
Making amend of my grey
Ways
And lonelier days
Your golden hello is
More than my end and
Beginning coming
Together.
I love you.
But then. I've said it
Already. And you know it.

Sunday
12th sept 2021

Grimsthorpe
I've come to find the God
In you. I've come to search
And seek the view
I came to see if it's true
That none knew love
Until they found you.
I've come to marvel at your grace
I've come to look upon your
Face.
I've come to see, experience
And taste
The wonder that is you.
I've come to marvel at your plan
I've come to seek and
Understand
I've come to stand in command
In the wonder that is you.
So I've come to you.
Dear Lord I've come to you.

I like you.
But then. That's easily said
And done if
We're both having fun
Lines upon lines of
Built friendship
And a shared view.
I like you.
Try not to take it offensively
Or personally if
None can gain from the
Information too.
But just a simple
Understanding and
Obsession with grace
I like staring at your face.
I like you.
And this view will never do
For a price
Less than eternity.

I've come for a slow stroll
With you.
A hand in hand
Cheek to cheek
Kind of walk
A meeting of old familiars
Originating from the
Same substance.
I've come to return to the
Essence and energy
That is you, O Most Divine.
And hoping that I find
Surprises within
Surprises
Myself again.
As it was in the beginning
Before the
Trouble started
With some bad fruit.

Everything is so still
And still I can
Find lots to thrill
With the knowing and
Acknowledgment of
You.
You mean to heal,
I mean to view
I'm being me
You just being you.
We let the sunlight
Through together
Whether, no one else
Is involved or not
Nor need to.

You've done some
Of your best works
Here Lord.
I see wonder in
Everything I do.
You've done some of
Your best works
Here Lord,
No-one can upstage
You
That much is true.
You've crafted some
Of your best
Here Lord
Never too late for one
To realize
Some of
Your finest and
Best Lord
And always
Welcome
Surprise.

I see the magic on
The lake.
I see divinity
For love's sake
I see the path this
Must take
To get back home to you.
I see the pristine
Glittering water
I see the sentences
That none dare
Utter
When they get this close
To you.
I see the science that
None can explain
I see the profit behind
Each gain.
Being one
With the view
I acknowledge and
Receive it
Being at one with you.

Little clumps of
Daises
Lining the path
You've created quite
an upstart
along the way.
No one can listen to
A word you say
When you look
The way you do.
You're simply
A ravishing
Sight for
Sore sights
When
No other sight
Will do.
Little clump of
daises
I adore you.

I missed writing to you
And about you
And wandering
Through you
And admiring you.
And exclaiming over
This and that
About you.
It's dreadful but it's
True
I shouldn't stay away
So long
Again in the future
To give you your
Due
You've always
Been
Unforgettable too.

The sun is high
The clouds are
Light
But autumn is
Coming and you
Know it.
O tree with the
Dappled
Shades of gold
Who told
You
So that you could
Start
Preparing
Yourself?
Was it a whisper
On the wind
Remnants from the
Original sin
Or all parts of God's
Plan
Dappled tree, preserver
Of energy. I like you.

I like your freshly
Turned earth.
I like to see
What can be
Made from dirt
And turned brand new.
What must the Creator
Make of you
With so much things to tell
Just as well.
You're like an open
Book.
And everywhere I look
The chance of something new
Coming through.
I like your freshly
Turned earth.
I really do.

Let me stay and
adore you.
Let me admire
Your greens
And hazels
And blue.
Even the grey
Headlining the
View is marvelous.
Let me stay with
You.
Let me sing praises
To and
About the view.
The splendor the
Wonder
Give the
Creator his due
Let me stay and
Worship
You.
I'm simply in love with you.

What does it take to
Make a tree
What blend what
Words
What symmetry?
What does it take
to make a
rose
The stems, the
Leaves
Do you suppose
The same Creator
That doth make
Me
Made the rose and
Also the tree
His perfect plan
For all to
See
And see and
See
Again.

You're not quite
Summer
But not quite
Winter
What are you?
You're not quite ready
To commit
To anything permanent
Either.
Green or gold
Take your pick
Autumn will have
Fun with you.

I can cope with a crown
Lord
I can cope with a crown
When all of this is
Over with and
The dusk is settling down
I can cope with a crown.
I can cope with despair Lord.
I can cope with despair
If you're really here
And not over there.
I can cope with despair.
I can cope with a race
Lord
I can cope with a race
If all I have to
Face is
Your triumphant right
Arm stretched out to
Grasp me at the end.
Then I can cope with a race
Too.
As long as I get to behold
Your face . Your wonderous
Wonderful face.
As long as I get to behold your face.

There's a God in me.
There's a God in you.
A God in every single
thing we do.
There's a God in the sky
God in the air
God in your moments
Of pain and despair
There's God in the shops.
God in your heart.
God when you stop.
God when you start.
God of new beginnings.
God of the old.
God in your down sitting.
God in your soul.
God in the azure, God in the
Blue. Please never
Forget the God in you.

19 September 2021

Autumn's
Coming.
And the trees run for cover
Shedding leaves
Quicker than you
Can say jumping jack
Lizards.
They have no time for
Dressing rooms
Or dress rehearsals
In their hurry.
Don't you worry
Yellow changes to
Brown
Soon enough and
Fall to the ground.
Leaving green a
Distant memory.
Autumn's coming
And there's no time for
Displays or the old
Ways of doing things
When winter is so hot on its heels.

Minute by minute
Hour by hour
The day gets sweeter
Just like a flower.
Second by second
Time after time
The heart has new
Beginnings
New rhythms and rhymes.
Sweeter and sweeter
It can be
Like midnight redemption
Eternity.
New beginnings
New horizons
New décor
Goodbye to old history
Past pains no more.
Fresh starts and
Flowers
Fresh chances to be
One with the Savior
And him with me.

You come to me in
silent whispers
like the very breath of
God.
You come with silence and
Sweetness and
Calmness
Taking nothing and
Wanting nothing in
Return.
For all my salty free
Yearnings
I yearn to be like you.
So free.
And open and loving
And giving.
I yearn for that breath from
God
To get started and
Restarted again.
I yearn for that
Refreshing dew
Anew from God.

Refreshing showers of rain
That allows us to
Begin as often and
Continuous as we
Want to.
Refreshing drops from heaven
That leaven
All the unsightly, unearthly
Bumps in our lives
Every time it goes
Pitter patter
Pitter on my head.

To Grimsthorpe

You look beautiful in
the rain.
Dewdrops on moist
Tall standing trees
Twinkling leaves
And falling yellows.
You look beautiful in
The rain.
With a youthful glow
And a river that flows
Towards all things
Graceful and abundant.
You look beautiful in
the mist
that hiss to announce
the arrival of you.
Never ordinary,
Never plain
You look beautiful in
The rain.
Soothing my pain.

....

Blank Page For Your Own Poem

Printed in the United States
by Baker & Taylor Publisher Services